The Right Balance: Harmony, Satisfaction, and Meaning in Life

Preface

Welcome to "The Right Balance: Harmony, Satisfaction, and Meaning in Life." This book is a journey through the concept of the Right Balance, a life philosophy that teaches us to find equilibrium in all spheres of our existence. Through the pages of this book, we will explore how the Right Balance can transform our lives, leading us to greater satisfaction, meaning, and well-being.

Modern life often pushes us toward extremes. We are bombarded with messages telling us to pursue success at any cost, to be constantly connected, and to attain unreachable standards of perfection. In this process, we risk losing sight of what is truly important: our happiness, well-being, and balance.

The Right Balance offers us an escape from this cycle of extremes. It teaches us to find a dynamic balance between opposites, to navigate the nuances of life, and to find the path to a more fulfilling and meaningful life. Through practical examples, inspiring stories, and concrete advice, this book will guide you on the journey to find your Right Balance in every aspect of your life.

You will learn how to apply the Right Balance in your career, interpersonal relationships, health and well-being, personal growth, ethics and morality, spiritual well-being, and global well-being. You will discover that there is no universal formula for the Right Balance but rather a unique path that is yours and yours alone.

We are excited to share this journey with you in the quest for balance, satisfaction, and meaning in life. We hope this book is a valuable resource that inspires you to find your Right Balance and live a more authentic and fulfilling life.

May this book guide you in your pursuit of the Right Balance and inspire you to create an extraordinary life every day. Bon voyage!

Chapter 1: Introduction

In the frantic race of modern life, we often find ourselves grappling with a persistent dilemma: how can we live a life that is fulfilling, meaningful, and, at the same time, balanced? In a world where extremes seem to dominate, finding "The Right Balance" may be the key to an extraordinary and happy life. This book is a journey to discover the power of balance and moderation in every aspect of life.

The idea of "The Right Balance" is an ancient and universal concept embraced by philosophers, thinkers, and cultures worldwide. It is a middle path that avoids extremes, a way towards a life that embraces diversity and harmony. It is not a compromise between good and evil but rather a thoughtful pursuit of balance between opposites.

In this book, we will explore the historical and philosophical origins of The Right Balance in various cultures, discover how to apply it to interpersonal relationships, career, health, personal growth, time management, ethics, and even spirituality. Each chapter will be an invitation to reflect on how The Right Balance can be applied in everyday life to achieve extraordinary results.

Readers will find in these pages a comprehensive guide that will help them find balance between ambition and fulfillment, between commitment and relaxation, between altruism and self-preservation. They will learn to navigate personal challenges with patience and wisdom, make ethical decisions based on moderation, and find a sense of inner peace through balanced spiritual exploration.

This book does not claim to offer magical solutions or rigid instructions but rather aims to provide a roadmap for the journey toward a special and fulfilling life. It is an invitation to explore The Right Balance and discover how to apply it practically to create a life where every day is a step towards bliss.

Let's prepare for a journey of self-exploration, personal growth, and realization. Let's discover together the power of The Right Balance and how it can transform our existence into something truly extraordinary. Are you ready to embark on this journey? Buckle up and get ready for an extraordinary adventure towards balance and happiness.

Chapter 2: Philosophical and Cultural Origins

In our journey to discover "The Right Balance," it is essential to understand the deep and cultural roots of this universal concept. The balance between opposites and the concept of The Right Balance has roots that delve into the history of philosophy and human culture. In this chapter, we will explore the origins and influences of The Right Balance in various philosophical and cultural traditions.

Greek Philosophy and Aurea Mediocritas

Let's begin our journey with ancient Greece, a civilization known for its profound philosophical reflections. Here, we find the concept of "Aurea Mediocritas" (or "Golden Mean"), which asserts that The Right

Balance is the point of equilibrium between extremes. Philosophers such as Aristotle, Plato, and Epicurus contributed to developing this concept. For instance, Aristotle emphasizes the importance of virtue as a balance between excess and deficiency.

In ancient Greece, the concept of The Right Balance was an essential part of ethics and philosophy, particularly thanks to the teachings of Aristotle. This philosophical principle underscored the importance of finding a virtuous balance between opposing extremes. Here's how The Right Balance was applied in the daily life of ancient Greece:

- **Aristotelian Virtues:** Aristotle identified various virtues, or habits of virtuous behavior, considered essential for leading an ethical and happy life. These virtues were often defined as The Right Balance between two extremes. For example, courage was considered The Right Balance between cowardice and recklessness, and generosity between stinginess and extravagance.

- **Citizens' Education:** In ancient Greece, the education of free citizens was fundamental to shaping virtuous individuals. Greek teachers and philosophers promoted the idea of The Right Balance as an integral part of education, teaching students how to behave with moderation and wisdom.

- **Politics and Philosophy:** The principle of The Right Balance was also present in the politics and philosophy of ancient Greece. The quest for balance between the power of the people (democracy) and the rule of a virtuous individual (monarchy) was a recurring theme in political discussions. Philosophers like Plato and Aristotle discussed ways to achieve a balanced form of government.

- **Art and Culture:** Even in art and culture, the concept of The Right Balance was evident. Greek tragedy often portrayed the consequences of a lack of moderation and excessive passion.

In summary, The Right Balance was a key component of the ethics and philosophy of ancient Greece. This principle influenced multiple aspects of daily life, from personal virtue to education, from politics to art, contributing to shaping the vision of balance and moderation in classical Greek society.

Chinese Philosophy and the Yin and Yang Concept

In Chinese philosophy, the concept of balance is embodied in the duality of Yin and Yang. The Right Balance is the result of harmony between these opposing forces. This concept has profound implications in traditional Chinese medicine, Confucian philosophy, and Taoism. We will explore how The Right Balance has been applied in daily life in China for centuries.

The concept of The Right Balance is a fundamental part of Chinese philosophy and has deeply influenced daily life in China for centuries. This principle is mainly found in the thoughts of Confucius and Taoism.

Here's how The Right Balance was applied in daily life in China:

- **Confucian Ethics:** Confucius taught the importance of finding The Right Balance in interpersonal and social relationships. This translates into a balance between familial duties, respect for elders, obedience to laws, and personal morality. In China, many social practices and ceremonies are based on these principles.

- **Taoism:** Taoism emphasizes the concept of "Wu Wei," translated as "action without action" or "going with the flow." This means seeking The Right Balance by following the natural flow of things and avoiding excessive action or interference. Taoism has influenced traditional Chinese medicine and martial arts, among other things.

- **Traditional Chinese Medicine:** Traditional Chinese Medicine applies The Right Balance in balancing Yin and Yang, the concepts of vital energy (Qi), and the use of herbs and therapeutic techniques to restore harmony in the body.

- **Culinary Culture:** Chinese cuisine often follows the principle of The Right Balance. The variety of dishes, ingredients, and cooking methods reflects the balance between the five flavors (sweet, bitter, sour, salty, spicy) and nutritional aspects.

- **Art and Philosophy:** Chinese art, calligraphy, and landscape painting often seek to represent the harmony and balance of The Right Balance. Chinese philosophy emphasizes the balance between complementary opposites, such as Yin and Yang.

In summary, The Right Balance is a philosophy deeply rooted in Chinese culture and daily life, influencing relationships, health, cuisine, arts, and much more. It is a principle that aims to promote harmony, balance, and wisdom in daily existence.

Other Cultural Traditions

Beyond Greece and China, the concept of The Right Balance has influenced cultures worldwide.

From Indian philosophies like Buddhism and Hinduism to Native American cultures and the African tradition of Ubuntu, we will discover how the need for balance is a universal trait of the human experience.

The search for balance and The Right Balance is a universal trait that spans various cultures and philosophical traditions worldwide. Let's explore how this search manifests in Indian philosophies like Buddhism and Hinduism, Native American cultures, and the African tradition of Ubuntu.

Buddhism (India):

Buddhism, born in India in the 6th century BCE with Siddhartha Gautama, shares the concept of The Right Balance through the Noble Eightfold Path. This path teaches the importance of finding balance between extremes such as desire and renunciation, anger and patience. Buddhism promotes wisdom and moderation as key to achieving liberation.

Hinduism (India):

Even in Hinduism, one of the world's oldest religions, the principle of The Right Balance is evident through the concept of "Dharma" (duties and obligations). Hinduism teaches that each individual must find a balance between social, familial, and spiritual duties to lead a harmonious life.

Native American Cultures:

Native American cultures often emphasize respect for nature and the balance between humans and the surrounding environment. The rituals and spiritual practices of Native American tribes incorporate the idea of The Right Balance in treating the earth with respect and seeking balance between humans and the natural world.

Ubuntu (Africa):

Ubuntu is an African philosophy that highlights the importance of interpersonal relationships, community, and sharing. In Ubuntu, the word "Ubuntu" itself means "we are because others are." This philosophy encourages the balance between individuality and community participation, promoting peace and harmony in society.
In summary, the need for balance and The Right Balance are universal concepts reflected in diverse cultures and traditions worldwide. These principles are fundamental to the pursuit of wisdom, harmony, and peace in various spheres of human life.

Practical Application

After exploring the philosophical and cultural origins of The Right

Balance, we will now consider
how we can apply this concept in
our daily lives. We will learn from
the wisdom of the past and see
how we can integrate these
lessons into our search for
balance and happiness.

Through this chapter, readers will
be invited to explore the cultural
heritage of humanity and
understand how The Right
Balance is a path to finding
equilibrium and wisdom in a world
often dominated by extremes. Our
journey into the world of
philosophical and cultural origins
of The Right Balance will give us a
more complete picture of this
concept and prepare us to apply
it successfully in our daily lives.
Are we ready to discover the deep
roots of The Right Balance and
how we can cultivate it to achieve

Chapter 3: The Right Balance in Interpersonal Relationships

Human relationships form the connective tissue of our existence. How we interact with others can profoundly impact our happiness and overall well-being. In this chapter, we will explore applying the concept of "The Right Balance" to our interpersonal relationships, revealing how we can cultivate deeper and more meaningful connections through balance and moderation.

Balancing Caring and Self-Care

In relationships, we often face the challenge of balancing caring for others with caring for ourselves. Too often, we find ourselves at opposite extremes: being overly altruistic and neglecting our needs or being selfish and neglecting others. Finding the Right Balance in this dynamic, learning to be present for others without losing sight of ourselves, is crucial.

Balanced Communication

Communication is fundamental in relationships. Too often, we find ourselves expressing too much or too little. We will explore how the Right Balance in communication can help us express our feelings and opinions in a balanced way, promoting mutual understanding and conflict resolution.

The practice of "The Right Balance" in communication plays a crucial role in fostering balanced expression of feelings and opinions, as well as promoting mutual understanding and conflict resolution. This approach is essential in various spheres of life, including personal

relationships, the workplace, and social interactions. Let's see how "The Right Balance" can be effectively applied:
Expressing Feelings with Empathy: The Right Balance involves expressing feelings openly but respectfully, avoiding extremes such as anger or emotional repression. Communicating feelings empathetically helps others understand our emotions.

Expressing Opinions with Respect: When sharing opinions, it's important to do so respectfully, avoiding accusatory or offensive tones. This fosters constructive dialogue instead of a defensive reaction.

Active Listening: Effective communication also involves actively listening to others. The Right Balance requires listening without interruptions, seeking to understand their perspectives.

Avoiding Generalizations: In seeking the Right Balance, let's avoid generalizations and stereotypes. Instead, focus on specific facts and concrete situations.

Resolving Conflicts

Constructively: In dealing with divergent opinions or managing conflicts, seeking the Right Balance means seeking balanced solutions that meet the needs of both parties.
Promoting Mutual Understanding: The ultimate goal is to promote mutual understanding. The Right Balance in communication helps build bridges rather than barriers between people.

In summary, applying "The Right Balance" in communication is a valuable skill for building healthy relationships and promoting understanding. This balanced approach can significantly contribute to conflict resolution and improvement of human interactions in various contexts.

Conflicts and Forgiveness

Every relationship has its conflicts. However, how we handle these conflicts can make the difference between breaking and strengthening relationships. We will learn to manage conflicts through moderation, seeking solutions that are fair to both parties. We will also explore the power of forgiveness in restoring balance in damaged relationships.

Forgiveness is an extraordinary force that can play a fundamental role in restoring balance in damaged relationships. Here's how forgiveness can positively influence relational dynamics: Reducing Distress and Bitterness: Forgiveness allows people to free themselves from the distress and bitterness associated with painful events or betrayals. This liberation contributes to restoring emotional balance.

Healing Emotional Wounds: Forgiveness offers an opportunity for the healing of emotional wounds. When forgiveness is extended, it opens the door to discussion and mutual understanding, allowing the involved parties to address and resolve issues.

Promoting Communication: Forgiveness fosters open and honest communication between the involved parties. This communication process can help identify the causes of conflicts and find shared solutions.

Reinforcing Emotional Bond: Forgiveness can strengthen the emotional bond between people. When a person forgives, they demonstrate a level of trust and compassion that can reinforce the connection with the other party.

Reducing Retaliation Cycle: In restoring balance, forgiveness breaks the cycle of retaliation. Instead of seeking revenge or perpetuating conflict, forgiveness paves the way for healing. Promoting Inner Peace: Forgiving can lead to greater inner peace. Letting go of anger and resentment can improve emotional and psychological well-being.

In summary, forgiveness is a powerful healing force that can significantly contribute to restoring balance in damaged relationships. Recognizing the power of forgiveness and actively seeking to forgive can lead to greater harmony and understanding in interpersonal relationships.

Boundaries and Emotional Connection

Establishing healthy boundaries is essential for well-being in relationships. However, too often, boundaries are confused with emotional detachment. We will explore how to set clear boundaries while maintaining a significant emotional connection with others.

Setting clear boundaries in relationships is crucial for maintaining a meaningful emotional connection with others. Here's how to do it:

Understand Your Needs: First and foremost, understand your needs, desires, and limits. This will help you define which boundaries are important to you.

Open Communication: Openly discuss the need to establish boundaries with others. Explain why it's important to you, and also listen to their opinions and feelings.
Be Aware of Emotions: Recognize your emotions and those of others during conversations about

boundaries. Be empathetic and try to understand how boundaries can influence the emotions of those involved.

Be Flexible: Boundaries are not rigid. They can evolve over time based on circumstances and needs. Be willing to review and update your boundaries when necessary.
Respect Others' Boundaries: It's equally important to respect the boundaries of others as it is to enforce your own. This will help create an environment of mutual trust.

Find a Balance: Seek a balance between setting boundaries and maintaining an emotional connection. There's no need to isolate yourself but rather find a way to protect your emotional well-being within the relationship.

Understand That Boundaries Are Healthy: Remember that setting boundaries is a sign of self-esteem and respect for yourself and others. It can lead to healthier and more satisfying relationships.

In summary, establishing clear boundaries is an important step in maintaining meaningful and healthy relationships. The key lies in open communication, empathy, and mutual respect.

Self-Love and Understanding

To fully understand relationships, we must first understand ourselves. We will explore how the Right Balance in self-reflection allows us to bring a better understanding of ourselves into relationships, creating deeper and more authentic bonds.

The concept of the "Right

Balance: according to Aristotle, represents a midpoint between extremes, an idea that can be applied in self-reflection and interpersonal relationships to promote a better understanding of oneself and create deeper and more authentic bonds.

Emotional Balance: Self-reflection allows us to explore our thoughts, emotions, and behaviors. Finding the right balance means avoiding excessive self-criticism on one hand and a lack of self-awareness on the other. This emotional balance promotes a more comprehensive understanding of oneself.

Empathy in Relationships: Applying the Right Balance to relationships involves seeking a balance between listening to others and expressing your own needs. This promotes mutual understanding and the creation of deeper bonds. Empathy, an integral part of the Right Balance, helps understand others' perspectives.

Avoiding Extremes: Excess or lack of self-reflection can lead to extreme behaviors in relationships, such as egocentrism or emotional dependence. Finding the right balance in self-reflection helps avoid such extremes, creating more authentic relationships.

Personal Growth: Targeted self-reflection aimed at the Right Balance can be a vehicle for personal growth. Understanding one's weaknesses and strengths allows for working on them in a balanced way, contributing to emotional maturity.

In summary, the Right Balance in self-reflection and relationships involves seeking a balance between emotional and behavioral extremes. This approach promotes a better understanding of oneself and others, creating deeper and more authentic connections based on empathy and personal growth.

Chapter 4: The Right Balance in Career and Ambition

Career and ambition are significant components of our lives, but often, we find ourselves caught between the pursuit of success and the desire for balance. In this chapter, we will explore how to apply the concept of "The Right Balance" to our careers and personal ambitions, discovering how to achieve professional goals without compromising overall well-being.

Striking a Balance between Ambition and Personal Fulfillment

The quest for success can become an endless race. We will learn to find the Right Balance between ambition and personal fulfillment, understanding that success should not necessarily translate to a hectic career or constant accumulation of wealth.

To find the Right Balance between ambition and personal fulfillment, it is essential to understand that success goes beyond a hectic career or the accumulation of material wealth. Here's how to do it:

- **Define Your Concept of Success:** Begin by reflecting on what success means to you personally. It might include career goals, but it should also consider your happiness, personal satisfaction, and emotional well-being.

- **Set Clear and Balanced Goals:** Once your concept of success is defined, set realistic and balanced goals covering various areas of your life, including career, family, health, and passion.

- **Prioritize and Manage Time:** Learn to prioritize your activities based on importance. Allocate time to things that matter most to you and be mindful of maintaining a work-life balance.

- **Flexibility and Adaptation:** Life is constantly evolving. Be flexible and open to adapting your goals and ambitions based on circumstances and your personal needs.

- **Maintain Emotional Balance:** Success should not jeopardize your emotional well-being. Learn to manage stress, keep an open mind, and develop resilience to face challenges.

- **Cultivate Meaningful Relationships:** Do not neglect interpersonal relationships while pursuing success. Human connections are fundamental for personal fulfillment. Dedicate time to your family, friends, and community.

- **Evaluate and Reflect:** Periodically, take time to assess your situation. Ask yourself if you are living in alignment with your values and personal goals.

- **Practice Gratitude:** Gratitude can help maintain a positive attitude while pursuing success. Appreciate what you have already achieved and be grateful for future opportunities.

Finding your Right Balance between ambition and personal

fulfillment is an individual process that requires self-reflection and adaptation. Remember that success is a path that should lead you to a meaningful and fulfilling life, not just to a hectic career or the accumulation of wealth.

Stress Management and Well-being at Work

Stress is an inevitable companion in our careers, but it can be managed in a balanced way. We will explore strategies for stress management that allow us to maintain a balance between work demands and our physical and mental well-being.

Managing stress and maintaining a balance between work demands and physical and mental well-being are crucial for a healthy and productive life. Here are some strategies that can help:

- **Practice Deep Breathing:** Deep breathing can help calm the mind and reduce stress. Dedicate a few minutes each day to breathe deeply and mindfully.

- **Regular Physical Activity:** Regular exercise is a powerful strategy for managing stress and promoting emotional well-being. Find an activity you enjoy and incorporate it into your routine.

- **Learn to Say No:** Do not be afraid to set limits and say no when necessary. Learn to manage others' expectations and focus on your priorities.

- **Time Management:** Use time management tools, such as a to-do list, to organize your work effectively. Plan regular breaks to rejuvenate.

- **Mindfulness Practice:**
  Mindfulness is a technique
  that helps you live in the
  present moment. It can
  help reduce anxiety and
  improve your
  concentration.

- **Maintain a Healthy Diet:**
  A balanced diet can
  influence your mood and
  energy. Eat nutritious foods
  and stay adequately
  hydrated.

- **Cultivate Interpersonal
  Relationships:** Positive
  relationships are important
  for well-being. Dedicate
  time to your family and
  friends and seek support
  when needed.

- **Learn to Delegate:** If you
  are in a leadership
  position, learn to delegate
  tasks to colleagues or

employees to reduce workload.

- **Schedule Time for Yourself:** Find time for yourself to engage in activities that relax and rejuvenate you, such as reading a book, taking a walk, or practicing a hobby.

- **Seek Professional Help:** If stress becomes overwhelming or negatively affects your mental health, consider consulting a psychologist or specialist for support.

Remember that there is no one-size-fits-all solution. Experiment with these strategies and adapt those that work best for you. Stress management and the balance between work and well-being require time and effort but are essential for a healthy and fulfilling life.

The Culture of Balance in Career

Many organizations are increasingly embracing a culture of work-life balance. We will explore how corporate policies and employers' attitudes can influence our work well-being and how we can seek opportunities that promote a healthy balance.

Corporate policies and employers' attitudes can have a significant impact on employees' work well-being. Here's how they affect well-being and how to seek opportunities to promote a healthy balance:

- **Flexibility Policies:** Companies offering flexible work policies, such as telecommuting or flexible hours, enable employees to better manage their time and personal commitments, promoting a balance between work and personal life.

- **Mental Well-being Support:** Companies promoting mental well-being programs, such as counseling or stress management training, demonstrate concern for employees' well-being.

- **Corporate Culture:** A company with a culture that values employee well-being creates an environment where individuals feel supported and can work more balanced.

- **Additional Benefits:** Company policies that include benefits such as comprehensive health insurance or paid personal leave enhance employees' overall well-being.

- **Personal Development Promotion:** Companies investing in employee training and personal development foster individual growth, contributing to well-being.

- **Open Communication:** A corporate culture of open communication and active listening can help address work-related concerns and employee issues effectively.

To seek opportunities that promote a healthy balance:

- **Evaluate Corporate Policies:** Research the policies and benefits offered by companies you are interested in working for and choose those that align with your work-life balance needs.

- **Ask Questions during Interviews:** During a job interview, inquire about corporate policies related to employee well-being to assess whether the company supports a healthy balance.

- **Use Internal Resources:** Utilize resources and programs offered by your employer to enhance your well-being, such as employee assistance programs or training.

- **Communicate Your Needs:** Openly communicate with your employer about your work-life balance needs. Many companies are willing to find solutions.

- **Evaluate Balance:** Periodically, assess your work-life balance and make adjustments if necessary. Balance is dynamic and may require adjustments over time.

In summary, corporate policies and employers' attitudes can significantly impact work well-being. Research opportunities and companies that support a healthy balance and openly communicate your needs to create a more rewarding work environment.

The Role of Passion and Interest in Career

The Right Balance in the career does not only mean achieving financial goals but also pursuing what we are passionate about. We will explore how we can find satisfaction in our careers through balancing duties and passions.

To find satisfaction in your career through the balance of duties and passions, it is important to follow some strategies:

- **Self-Awareness:** Begin with a self-assessment of your passions and abilities. What excites you? What are your core skills? Knowing yourself is crucial to finding a job that satisfies you.

- **Career Choice:** Look for career opportunities that align with your passions. If you love what you do, you will naturally be more motivated and satisfied.

- **Flexibility:** Look for ways to incorporate your passions into your current career or job. You might be able to develop projects or roles that involve what you love.

- **Work-Life Balance:** Find a balance between your work and personal life. Dedicate time to your passions outside of the work environment to maintain balance.

- **Continuous Development:** Invest in your professional development. Acquiring new skills or honing existing ones can open up new career opportunities more in line with your passions.

- **Communication with the Employer:** Talk to your employer if you want to make changes to your role or career to align them with your passions. Some employers are open to discussions about customized roles.

- **Networking:** Attend networking events to connect with people who share your passions or work in related fields.

- **Financial Planning:** Consider the financial aspect when trying to balance duties and passions. You might need to make some financial choices or plan for a gradual transition.

- **Maintain Motivation:** Even when working in your passions, there will be challenges. Maintain motivation and commitment to overcome obstacles.

- **Personal Fulfillment:** Finally, remember that personal fulfillment is not only tied to your career.

Time spent with family, friends, and hobbies can significantly contribute to your overall happiness.

Find the balance between duties and passions to create a satisfying career and fulfilling life. Explore opportunities that allow you to cultivate what you love and engage in work that gives you a sense of accomplishment.

Balancing Time between Work and Personal Life

Time is a precious asset. We will find ways to balance time dedicated to work with that reserved for personal life, creating space for interests, relationships, and relaxation.
To balance time dedicated to work with that reserved for personal life, creating space for interests, relationships, and relaxation, here are some effective ways:

- **Set Priorities:** Identify the most important activities and obligations both on the work and personal fronts. Prioritize what is essential to you.

- **Time Management:** Use time management techniques like daily planning, task lists, and scheduling activities in dedicated time blocks.

- **Set Limits:** Be assertive in defining boundaries between work and personal life. Establish a regular work schedule and respect break times.

- **Delegate and Seek Help:** If possible, delegate tasks at work or home. Ask for help from colleagues or family when needed.

- **Quality Time:** Dedicate quality time to family,

friends, and activities you love. Be present during these interactions.

- **Continuous Learning:** Invest in yourself through continuous training and personal development. This can improve your work efficiency and increase career opportunities.

- **Relaxation and Self-Care:** Plan moments for relaxation and self-care. Physical exercise, meditation, reading, or any activity that helps you relax.

- **Clear Communication:** Communicate clearly with your employer, colleagues, and family about your work-life balance needs. Clear communication can prevent overload and stress.

- **Flexibility:** Look for job opportunities that offer flexibility, such as telecommuting or flexible hours, if possible.

- **Maintain Interests:** Do not neglect your personal interests. Cultivate your passions and hobbies, as they can bring satisfaction and well-being.

- **Family Schedule:** If you have a family, create a family schedule where each member can share their activities and commitments.

- **Vacations and Breaks:** Plan regular breaks and vacations to disconnect from work and recharge.

Balancing work and personal life is essential for maintaining good mental health, satisfying relationships, and a fulfilling life. Adopt these strategies to create space for yourself, the interests you love, and relaxation, thereby improving the overall quality of your life.

The Importance of Flexibility and Adaptability

The world of work is constantly evolving. We will learn the importance of adaptability and flexibility in pursuing a balanced career, allowing us to face challenges resiliently. Adaptability and flexibility are crucial qualities for pursuing a balanced career and facing challenges resiliently. Here's why they are so important:

- **Responding to Challenges:** Careers often involve changes, challenges, and unexpected events. Being flexible allows you to adapt quickly to new situations and find creative solutions to problems.

- **Professional Growth:** Being open to change and willing to learn new skills makes you a more well-rounded and adaptable professional. This can increase your opportunities for career growth and advancement.

- **Resilience:** Flexibility is a key component of resilience. It means having the ability to overcome obstacles and bounce back quickly from difficulties. This skill is essential for maintaining mental and emotional stability during stressful times.

- **Evolving Work Environment:** Today, workplaces are changing faster than ever due to technology and business dynamics. Being flexible helps you thrive in a rapidly evolving environment.

- **Work-Life Balance:** Flexibility allows you to manage your time better and create a balance between work and personal life. This is crucial for maintaining overall well-being.

- **Competitiveness:** Professionals who demonstrate adaptability are often considered more valuable by companies. They can handle a variety of tasks and situations, making them competitive in the job market.

- **Personal Growth:** Embracing change fosters personal growth. It allows you to explore new opportunities and discover hidden passions.

In summary, adaptability and flexibility are crucial for a balanced career and resiliently facing challenges. These qualities not only enhance your professional prospects but also contribute to your overall well-being, enabling you to thrive in an ever-evolving world.

This chapter is a journey into the art of pursuing professional success without sacrificing the quality of life. We will learn to define success more broadly, find a balance between ambition and well-being, and create a career that is authentic and fulfilling. The Right Balance in the career is a path toward meaningful work and a satisfying life. Are you ready to discover how to pursue your ambition in a balanced and fulfilling manner?

Career and ambition are integral parts of many of our lives. Pursuing our professional goals can lead to the realization of dreams and aspirations, but it can also become fertile ground for anxiety, stress, and inequality. The Right Balance teaches us how to pursue success without losing sight of who we are.

Often, in the quest for professional success, we fall into the trap of hyper-competitiveness. We push ourselves beyond limits, sacrificing our time, health, and relationships to advance in our careers. However, the Right Balance reminds us that success should not mean the decline of our personal well-being. Instead, we can set ambitious goals while staying grounded in our values and authenticity.

An essential part of applying the Right Balance in the career is time and priority management. Learning to set priorities and adopting strategic planning can help us maintain a balance between work and personal life. This also emphasizes the importance of disconnecting when necessary, taking breaks, and moments of relaxation to rejuvenate the mind and body. The Right Balance also teaches us to embrace flexibility. Life is unpredictable, and unexpected changes and challenges can occur in our careers. The ability to adapt to circumstances and find creative solutions can be a valuable asset.

In the pursuit of success, it's crucial to consider what sacrifices we are willing to make and whether those sacrifices will truly be rewarding in the long run. The Right Balance encourages reflection on our definition of success and evaluating whether we are pursuing goals that align with our values and overall well-being.

Lastly, the importance of relationships and sharing success should not be overlooked. The Right Balance teaches us to celebrate our achievements with others and build meaningful connections in our professional lives.

In the next chapter, we will explore how the Right Balance can be applied to our physical well-being, showing how to maintain a balance between body care and the fulfillment of our desires. But first, reflect on your career and ambitions. How can you apply the Right Balance to pursue success without losing yourself?

Chapter 5: Striking the Right Balance in Health and Well-being

Our health and well-being are crucial for leading a fulfilling and energetic life. However, we often find ourselves navigating extremes in our approach to health, swinging between excess and neglect. In this chapter, we will explore how to apply the concept of "The Right Balance" to our health and well-being, aiming to live a balanced and vibrant life.

Balanced Diet

Nutrition is a crucial aspect of our health, and The Right Balance applies here as well. We will explore adopting a balanced diet, avoiding both excessive junk food consumption and excessive restriction. We will learn the art of mindful eating and listening to our bodies.

To adopt a balanced diet and avoid both excessive junk food consumption and excessive restriction, it's important to follow some fundamental principles that promote the art of mindful eating and listening to our bodies:

- **Balancing Food Groups:** A balanced diet should include a variety of foods from different food groups, including proteins, carbohydrates, healthy fats, fruits, vegetables, and dairy or alternatives. Maintaining a balance among these groups ensures that the body receives all the necessary nutrients to function properly.

- **Moderation:** not Deprivation: Avoid excessive restriction. Occasionally eating junk food or indulging in a meal outside your usual diet is acceptable. The key is moderation and balance overall.

- **Listen to Your Body:** Learn to recognize your body's signals of hunger and fullness. Eat when you're hungry and stop when you're satisfied. Don't be influenced by fixed schedules or emotions.

- **Meal Planning:** Prepare meals in advance to avoid resorting to junk food for convenience. Planning allows you to have healthy foods readily available.

- **Avoid Extreme Diets:** Steer clear of extreme or restrictive diets that may lead to nutritional deficiencies or an unhealthy relationship with food.

- **Choose Healthy Options:** When craving a snack, opt for healthier alternatives to junk food, such as fruits, nuts, or Greek yogurt.

- **Read Labels:** Familiarize yourself with the nutritional labeling of foods. Look for foods with simple and nutritious ingredients.

- **Hydration:** Ensure you drink enough water throughout the day. Sometimes thirst can be confused with hunger.

- **Food Awareness:** Eat slowly, savoring each bite. This helps avoid overeating and promotes full food awareness.

- **Support and Consultation:** If you encounter difficulties adopting a balanced diet, consider consulting a nutritionist or dietitian for personalized guidance.

- **Remember that:** the key to a healthy diet is finding a balance that works for you, listening to your body, and making mindful food choices. There's no one-size-fits-all diet, but by following these principles, you can approach a balanced and sustainable eating regimen over time.

Moderate Physical Exercise

Physical activity is important for both physical and mental well-being. However, excessive training can lead to injuries and stress, while lack of exercise can cause health problems. We will explore finding the Right Balance in physical training, adopting a balanced approach to staying fit.

To find the right balance in physical training and maintain

fitness, it's essential to adopt a balanced approach that takes into account various factors. Here's how to do it:

- **Planning and Realistic Goals:** Start with proper planning. Set realistic goals that consider your current fitness level and the time you can dedicate to training. Find a balance between ambition and realism.

- **Variety in Training:** Avoid boredom and the risk of overtraining by introducing variety into your workouts. Combining different activities like cardio, weightlifting, yoga, and stretching can keep training interesting.

- **Adequate Rest:** Recovery is crucial. Don't overload your body, and allow rest days between intense sessions. Quality sleep is equally important for recovery.

- **Listening to Your Body:** Learn to listen to your body. If you feel pain or excessive fatigue, slow down or take a break. Listening to your body prevents injuries and overtraining.

- **Balanced Nutrition:** Training and diet are interconnected. Maintain a balanced diet with proteins, carbohydrates, and healthy fats. Avoid excesses and follow your calorie needs.

- **Consistency:** Consistency is key. Maintain a regular workout routine in the long term, rather than intense efforts followed by periods of inactivity.

- **Active Recovery:** Include active recovery activities such as stretching, muscle relaxation, or massage to improve flexibility and prevent injuries.

- **Mind-Body Balance:** Physical exercise is not just about the body but also the mind. Practice relaxation and meditation to reduce stress and improve mental well-being.

- **Consultation with a Professional:** If you're new to training or have specific goals, consider consulting a fitness professional or a personal trainer for a personalized plan.

- **Enjoy the Process:** Finally, remember that training should be enjoyable. Find physical activities you like that keep you motivated in the long run.

- **Maintaining:** a balance in physical exercise requires time, patience, and self-awareness. By adopting a balanced approach, you can sustain fitness and enjoy long-term benefits.

Stress Management and Mental Health

Mental health is as important as physical health. We will learn how to manage stress and promote mental well-being through practices like meditation, mindfulness, and emotional balance.
Managing stress and promoting mental well-being are important goals for maintaining optimal psychophysical health. Here's how you can do it through practices like meditation, mindfulness, and emotional balance:

- **Meditation:** Meditation is a practice that helps calm the mind, reduce stress, and improve concentration. Find a quiet place, sit comfortably, and focus your attention on an object, sound, or your own breath. Regular meditation can promote inner calm and mental clarity.

- **Mindfulness:** Mindfulness is awareness of the present moment. It involves deliberate attention to what you are doing without judgment. You can practice it in many daily activities, such as eating, walking, or even working. Mindfulness helps reduce anxiety, improve emotional awareness, and promote resilience.

- **Emotional Balance:** Find emotional balance by managing emotions in a healthy way. This includes expressing emotions appropriately, dealing with your feelings, and using coping strategies like art, writing, or talking to a friend or therapist.

- **Physical Activity:** Physical exercise is a powerful ally for mental well-being. Physical activity releases endorphins, brain chemicals that enhance mood and reduce stress. Find a physical activity you enjoy and make it a part of your routine.

- **Balanced Diet:** A healthy and balanced diet contributes to mental well-being. Consume nutrient-rich foods like fruits, vegetables, lean proteins, and healthy fats. Avoid excess sugar and caffeine, which can negatively impact mood.

- **Adequate Sleep:** Quality sleep is crucial for mental well-being. Establish a regular sleep routine and aim for 7-9 hours of sleep per night.

- **Stress Management Techniques:** Learn stress management techniques such as deep breathing, yoga, or the practice of gratitude. These practices help reduce tension and maintain a positive outlook.

- **Social Support:** Talk to friends and family when facing stressful situations. Sharing your thoughts and feelings can alleviate the burden of stress.

- **Professional Therapy:** In case of more severe or persistent mental health issues, consider consulting a psychotherapist or psychiatrist for professional support.

- **Time for Yourself:** Dedicate time for yourself every day. Be kind to yourself and engage in activities that relax and recharge you.

- **Managing:** stress and promoting mental well-being require constant practice and commitment, but the rewards for your mental and physical health are undoubtedly worth it.

Restful Sleep

Sleep is fundamental for our well-being, yet it is often neglected. We will explore how to find the Right Balance in sleep, adopting healthy sleep routines and ensuring quality rest.

To achieve the right balance in sleep and ensure quality rest, it's essential to adopt a healthy sleep routine. Here are some tips to do so:

- **Set a Fixed Schedule:** Try to go to bed and wake up at the same time every day, even on days off. This helps regulate your circadian rhythm and improve sleep quality.

- **Create a Comfortable Environment:** Ensure your sleep environment is dark, quiet, and cool. Use blackout curtains and earplugs if necessary. A good mattress and comfortable pillows are also crucial.

- **Limit Caffeine and Alcohol:** Avoid consuming caffeine and alcohol, especially in the evening. These substances can interfere with sleep and cause sleep disturbances.

- **Physical Exercise:** Regular physical activity can improve sleep quality, but avoid exercising too close to bedtime. Try to finish your workout at least 3 hours before sleeping.

- **Limit Evening Food Intake:** Avoid heavy meals and fatty snacks before bedtime. A small, light snack may be helpful if you're hungry, but avoid large meals before sleep.

- **Relaxation Before Bed:** Before going to bed, allocate time for relaxation. You can read a book, take a warm shower, or practice meditation to calm the mind and prepare for sleep.

- **Limit Blue Light Exposure:** Avoid electronic devices like smartphones, tablets, and computers before sleep, as they emit blue light that can interfere with melatonin production, the sleep hormone.

- **Avoid Prolonged Daytime Napping:** If you take a nap during the day, try to limit it to 20-30 minutes to avoid interfering with nighttime sleep.

- **Consult a Specialist:** If you have persistent sleep difficulties, you may want to consult a sleep specialist to evaluate any sleep disorders.

- **Keep a Sleep Diary:**
  Keeping a sleep diary can
  help monitor your sleep
  patterns and identify any
  issues. This can be useful
  when trying to improve
  sleep quality.

- **Achieving:** the right
  balance in sleep requires
  consistency and discipline
  in your routine. By
  adopting these healthy
  practices, you can
  promote quality rest and
  enhance your overall
  health.

Avoiding Extremes in Healthy Behaviors

Avoiding extremes is not only
about diet and exercise but also
about steering clear of harmful
behaviors like alcohol abuse,
smoking, or screen addiction. We
will explore how to find a healthy
balance in these areas of life.

To find a healthy balance in life, it's important to consider different key areas and adopt appropriate strategies in each of them. Here are some recommendations to achieve a healthy balance in various life areas:

- **Work-Life Balance:** Find a balance between work and leisure. Set clear working hours and try to stick to them. Dedicate time to activities you are passionate about outside of work.

- **Physical Health:** Maintain an active lifestyle and a balanced diet. Engage in regular physical activity, consume nutritious foods, and ensure you get sufficient rest.

- **Mental Health:** Take care of your mental health. Practice meditation, mindfulness, or activities that help you relax and manage stress. Talk to a mental health professional if needed.

- **Interpersonal Relationships:** Cultivate meaningful relationships with friends and family. Allocate time for loved ones and strive to maintain a balance between personal and social relationships.

- **Personal Growth:** Invest in yourself through continuous learning and personal growth. Read books, take courses, or try new activities that challenge you and contribute to your growth.

- **Time for Yourself:** Find moments of solitude and reflection. This time for yourself can help you better understand yourself and recharge.

- **Goals and Passions:** Identify your goals and passions in life. Make a plan to gradually achieve them and maintain a balance between pursuing these goals and enjoying the present.

- **Time Management:** Learn to manage your time effectively. Prioritize important activities and learn to say "no" when necessary.

- **Social Contributions:** Look for ways to give back to the community or society. Volunteering or helping others can bring a sense of fulfillment and accomplishment.

- **Hobbies and Interests:**
  Cultivate your hobbies and
  interests. These activities
  can be an important
  source of joy and balance
  in life.

- **Remember that:** life
  balance can vary from
  person to person, and
  what is balanced for you
  may not be the same for
  someone else. It's
  important to listen to
  yourself, regularly assess
  your life, and make
  necessary changes to
  maintain a healthy and
  fulfilling balance.

Prevention and Self-Care

Prevention is often overlooked but
essential for our long-term health.
We will explore adopting a
proactive mindset towards our
health and well-being, seeking the
Right Balance between neglect
and hypochondria.

This chapter invites you to explore how finding the Right Balance in health and well-being can lead to a healthier, more energetic, and more satisfying life. We will learn to avoid extremes in the pursuit of health, adopting a balanced approach that allows us to fully enjoy life. The Right Balance in health is the key to a vibrant and fulfilling life. Are you ready to discover how to achieve this balance in your life?

Stress is an inevitable companion in all our lives. Daily challenges, work pressures, worries, and uncertainties can accumulate and test our mental and emotional health. However, the Right Balance offers an approach to address stress in a balanced way, allowing us to maintain mental serenity even in the most challenging situations.

The art of managing stress through the Right Balance begins with awareness. Often, we are so immersed in our thoughts and worries that we lose connection with the present moment. Mindfulness, or awareness, is a practice that teaches us to be present and observe our thoughts and emotions without judgment. This allows us to approach stress in a calmer and more effective manner.

One of the keys to applying the Right Balance in stress management is recognizing our limits. Often, we push ourselves too far, trying to cope with too many responsibilities or commitments. The result is a feeling of overwhelm and anxiety. The Right Balance teaches us to say "enough" when necessary, to set priorities, and to delegate when possible.

Stress management through the Right Balance also involves finding time for ourselves and activities that rejuvenate us. Constantly working without breaks can lead to physical and emotional exhaustion. The Right Balance encourages us to give ourselves time for rest, relaxation, and personal enjoyment.

Another crucial aspect of stress management is realistic optimism. The Right Balance teaches us to prepare for the worst but hope for the best. This approach helps us avoid excessive worry and maintain a positive perspective even in challenging circumstances.

Lastly, social support is an important element in stress management. Sharing concerns with friends, family, or a mental health professional can alleviate the burden of stress and provide valuable perspectives.

In the next chapter, we will explore the Right Balance in career and ambition, showing how we can pursue our professional goals without sacrificing our health and well-being. But first, reflect on stress in your life. How can you apply the Right Balance to manage stress more equitably and maintain mental serenity?

Chapter 6: The Right Balance in Personal Growth

Personal growth is a journey of continuous self-evolution and improvement. However, it can be challenging to find the balance between the ambition to grow and maintaining overall well-being in daily life. In this chapter, we will explore how to apply the concept of "The Right Balance" to personal growth, to achieve personal development goals without losing sight of overall well-being.

Realistic and Sustainable Goals

The key to sustainable personal growth is setting realistic goals. We will learn to define goals that are ambitious yet achievable, avoiding frustration and burnout. Setting ambitious yet achievable goals is crucial to avoid frustration and burnout. Here's how to do it:

- **Break down goals into stages:** Rather than setting a massive single goal, break it down into smaller, manageable objectives. This makes the path to the final goal less intimidating and more rewarding with each small progress.

- **Be realistic:** Evaluate your resources, available time, and current abilities carefully. Ensure the goals you set are realistic based on these considerations. It's important to challenge yourself without jeopardizing your well-being.

- **Maintain flexibility:** Life is unpredictable. At times, you may need to adapt your goals to new circumstances or opportunities. Don't be afraid to make changes when necessary.

- **Set reasonable deadlines:** Establish deadlines that are realistic and sustainable. Avoid overloading yourself with overly tight timelines for goals.

- **Measure and celebrate progress:** Keep track of your progress toward your goals. This helps you see how close you are to achieving success. And don't forget to celebrate small victories along the way.

- **Seek support:** If you feel overwhelmed or frustration arises, seek support from friends, family, or professionals. Sharing your challenges and receiving advice can be extremely helpful.

- **Practice self-compassion:** Don't be too hard on yourself if things don't go exactly as planned. Perfection is not always possible. Accept obstacles and challenges as opportunities for growth.

- **Review and adapt:** Periodically review your goals and progress. This allows you to make any necessary changes based on your experiences and growth.

In summary, defining ambitious yet achievable goals requires planning, realism, and flexibility. This approach will help you maintain high motivation and prevent frustration and burnout in the pursuit of your personal growth goals.

Patience and Persistence

Personal growth requires time and consistent effort. We will explore the importance of patience and persistence in pursuing change and self-improvement.
Patience and persistence play a crucial role in pursuing change and self-improvement. Here's why they are important:

- **Gradual progress:** Personal change and improvement take time. Patience allows you to face challenges gradually, without expecting immediate results. It's essential to accept that progress won't always be linear and constant.

- **Resilience:** Persistence is the ability to keep working toward a goal despite obstacles and difficulties. In the process of personal change, there will be tough moments. Persistence helps you overcome them rather than giving up.

- **Learning:** Patience enables learning from mistakes and experiences. Change requires adaptation and continuous improvement, and patience allows you to face challenges as opportunities for growth.

- **Lasting achievement:** Quick results can be gratifying but often short-lived. Patience and persistence lead to more lasting and meaningful results over time.

- **Consistency:** Personal change requires consistent actions over time. Patience and persistence help you maintain consistency in your actions and develop positive habits.

- **Self-control:** Patience instills self-control and self-regulation. These skills are crucial for overcoming temptations and distractions that may hinder your personal improvement journey.

- **Improved self-esteem:** Overcoming challenges and achieving goals through patience and persistence increases self-confidence and self-esteem.

In summary, patience and persistence are vital qualities for personal change and self-improvement. They allow you to face challenges, learn from failures, and achieve significant and lasting results in the pursuit of your personal growth goals.

Balancing Comfort and Challenge

To grow, we must push ourselves outside our comfort zone. However, it's important to find the Right Balance between comfort and challenge, avoiding excessive anxiety and stress.
To grow and develop one's potential, it's crucial to step out of the comfort zone. However, it's equally important to find a balance between comfort and challenge to avoid excessive anxiety and stress. Here's how to do it:

- **Gradual progression:** Start slowly by expanding the boundaries of your comfort zone. Face light challenges initially and gradually increase complexity. This allows you to acclimate to change without feeling it as a sudden disruption to your routine.

- **Realistic goals:** Set ambitious but achievable goals. This will motivate you to push beyond your comfort zone without inducing anxiety. Unattainable goals can cause stress.

- **Self-awareness:** Know your limits and listen to your body and mind. If you feel signs of excessive stress, slow down and assess if you're pushing too hard. Self-awareness will help you maintain control.

- **Resilience:** Accept that there will be challenging moments and times when you might fail. Resilience helps you face these challenges without being overwhelmed by anxiety.

- **Meditation and mindfulness:** Practice meditation and mindfulness to manage stress and stay centered during change. These techniques can help you remain calm.

- **Self-care:** Ensure you take care of yourself physically and mentally during the growth process. Adequate rest, physical exercise, and a balanced diet are essential.

- **Continuous reflection:** Periodically reflect on your progress and situation. This will help you adjust the pace and adapt your strategy based on your needs.

- **Social support:** Seek support from friends, family, or a professional if you feel overwhelmed.

Sharing your challenges can lighten the burden.

In conclusion, stepping out of the comfort zone is crucial for personal growth, but it's equally important to do so in a balanced way to avoid excessive anxiety and stress. Finding the "Right Balance" requires self-awareness, realistic goals, and self-care.

Reflection and Self-Awareness

Personal growth also requires reflection and self-awareness. We will learn to recognize our strengths and weaknesses and use this awareness to guide growth.
Recognizing our strengths and weaknesses is crucial for guiding personal growth. Here's how you can do it:

- **Self-assessment:** Dedicate time to honest self-assessment. Reflect on what you do well and what you could improve. Also, seek feedback from trusted individuals.

- **SWOT analysis:** Use the SWOT analysis (Strengths, Weaknesses, Opportunities, Threats) to identify your strengths and weaknesses. This tool will help you gain a clear view of yourself.

- **Active listening:** Pay attention to how you react in different situations. What excites you, and what scares you? These are signals of your strengths and weaknesses.

- **External feedback:** Accept honest feedback from colleagues, friends, and family. Sometimes, others see aspects of you that you may not recognize on your own.

- **Progressive growth:** After identifying weaknesses, look for opportunities for improvement. Learn new skills or work on existing ones.

- **Emphasize strengths:** Highlight your strengths in your daily activities. Leverage them for success and satisfaction.

- **Realistic goals:** When planning growth goals, consider your strengths and weaknesses. Set realistic goals that challenge you without being unattainable.

- **Self-care:** During the growth process, take care of yourself physically and mentally. General well-being enhances your ability to grow.

- **Continuous monitoring:** Periodically reassess your strengths and weaknesses as they can evolve over time. Maintain an open attitude toward change.

- **Support:** Seek support from mentors, coaches, or therapists if you feel you need external help to address your challenges.

Recognizing and utilizing awareness of your strengths and weaknesses is an essential step toward personal growth and success in every area of life.

Time and Priority Management

Too often, we overload ourselves with commitments and activities, making it challenging to focus on personal growth. We will explore how to manage time and priorities to make room for our evolution.

Managing time and priorities is crucial to making room for personal growth. Here's how to do it:

- **Daily planning:** Start the day by planning what you need to do. Make a list of tasks to complete and assign them priorities.

- **Eisenhower Matrix:** Use the Eisenhower Matrix to distinguish between urgent and important tasks. Focus on important activities that contribute to your growth.

- **Delegation:** If possible, delegate less important or repetitive tasks to others, allowing you to concentrate on what truly matters for your development.

- **Set long-term goals:**
Define clear long-term
goals for your personal
growth. These goals
provide direction and help
you make priority-based
decisions.

- **Flexibility:** Be flexible in
managing your time.
Sometimes, you need to
adapt to unforeseen
situations or unexpected
opportunities that can
contribute to your growth.

- **Learn to say "no":** You
don't need to accept every
request or commitment.
Learn to say "no" to what
is not fundamental for your
personal development.

- **Take regular breaks:**
Ensure you take breaks
during the day to
rejuvenate. A fresh mind is
more effective in time
management.

- **Use time management tools:** Numerous tools and apps, such as Trello or Asana, can help you organize activities and priorities.

- **Self-reflection:** Periodically reflect on your time use. Ask yourself if you're investing time in areas that genuinely contribute to your growth.

- **Continuous learning:** Dedicate time to continuous learning. Acquiring new knowledge and skills is a key element for personal evolution.

By effectively managing time and prioritizing activities that contribute to your growth, you will create the necessary space to evolve and achieve your personal goals.

Self-Acceptance and Compassion

Personal growth should not be an obsessive self-improvement process. We will learn the importance of self-acceptance and compassion in the growth journey.

This chapter is a journey into the art of balanced personal growth. We will learn to cultivate a mindset of constant improvement without falling into hyper-perfectionism or the escape from balance. The Right Balance in personal growth is the key to becoming the best version of oneself without sacrificing well-being and happiness. Are you ready to start this journey of self-exploration and balanced improvement?

Personal and spiritual growth is an intrinsic journey for every human being. It is the quest for knowledge, awareness, and meaning that enriches our inner life. The Right Balance in this context invites us to balance the desire for growth with inner peace and serenity.

In our hectic era, we are often driven to pursue personal growth incessantly, as if we constantly need to improve. However, this approach can lead to a constant feeling of dissatisfaction and perpetual anxiety. The Right Balance teaches us to cultivate personal growth in a balanced way, appreciating our progress without ever feeling incomplete.

Personal growth can take many forms, from continuous learning and reading to pursuing new skills and passions. The Right Balance lies in finding the right equilibrium between the desire to grow and accepting ourselves as we are. Embracing our authenticity and not judging our worth solely based on achievements is crucial.

The spiritual dimension is another aspect of personal growth that the Right Balance can enrich. The search for meaning and connection with something greater than ourselves is an essential part of life for many. The Right Balance in this context teaches us to explore spirituality openly and respectfully of different perspectives, avoiding religious extremism or complete lack of spirituality.

The practice of meditation and mindfulness can be a valuable tool for cultivating personal and spiritual growth through the Right Balance. These practices help us develop self-awareness, allowing us to deepen our understanding and connection with the profound reality.

An attitude of gratitude is a key element of personal and spiritual growth through the Right Balance. Being grateful for what we have in life, for the lessons learned from challenges, and for daily joys can profoundly enrich our inner journey.

In the next chapter, we will explore the Right Balance in living in the present, showing how we can enjoy every moment without losing sight of the past or the future.
But first, reflect on your personal and spiritual growth. How can you apply the Right Balance to cultivate your knowledge, awareness, and meaning without losing inner peace?

Chapter 7: The Right Balance in Time Management

Time is a precious and limited resource, and how we manage it can have a profound impact on our lives. Too often, we find ourselves struggling with the feeling of having too much to do and too little time. In this chapter, we will explore how to apply the concept of "The Right Balance" in time management to maximize productivity and well-being without succumbing to anxiety and stress.

Effective Prioritization

One of the pillars of time management is the ability to set priorities. We will learn to identify the most important tasks and focus on them, avoiding wasting time on less meaningful activities. To identify and concentrate on the most important tasks while avoiding wasting time on less meaningful ones, you can follow these steps:

- **Planning:** Start each day or week with a plan. Make a list of the tasks you need to address.

- **Prioritization:** Evaluate each task based on its importance. Ask yourself which tasks will contribute most to your long-term goals.

- **Eisenhower Matrix:** Use the Eisenhower Matrix, which categorizes tasks into four categories: Urgent and Important, Urgent but Not Important, Important but Not Urgent, Not Important and Not Urgent. Focus on the first category.

- **Clear Goals:** Ensure you have clear long-term goals. These will help you better identify priority tasks.

- **Delegation:** If possible, delegate less important tasks to others to free up time for what truly matters.

- **Eliminate Distractions:** Reduce distractions like phone notifications or social media while working on important tasks.

- **Flexibility:** Maintain some flexibility in your schedule to adapt to unforeseen situations, but don't let less significant tasks take over.

- **Self-Evaluation:** Periodically assess how you're managing your time. Ask yourself if your activities align with your goals.

- **Continuous Learning:** Develop your ability to recognize what is truly important for you and your success.

- **Celebrate Progress:** Acknowledge your successes when completing important tasks. This will motivate you to continue focusing on what matters.

By following these steps, you will be able to identify and concentrate on the most important tasks, avoiding wasting time on less meaningful ones and contributing to your personal and professional success.

Balance Between Work and Personal Life

The right balance between work and personal life is essential for overall well-being. We will explore strategies to balance career demands with time dedicated to family, hobbies, and relaxation. Balancing the demands of your career, family, hobbies, and relaxation is essential for a satisfying and fulfilling life. Here are some strategies to help you find this balance:

- **Planning:** Create a weekly or monthly plan that includes time dedicated to your career, family, hobbies, and relaxation. This will help you visualize how you are allocating your time.

- **Prioritization:** Identify your priorities in each area of life. What is most important to you? Make sure to dedicate more time to your priorities.

- **Delegation:** If possible, delegate some responsibilities on the career or home front to free up time for other activities.

- **Communication:** Communicate with your family or partner about your work needs and the times you want to be with them. Open communication can help avoid conflicts.

- **Quality Time:** When with family or engaged in hobbies, focus on the quality of time rather than quantity.

- **Limit Distractions:** Reduce distractions at work to be more productive, so you can finish earlier and spend time with family or engage in hobbies.

- **Self-Care:** Do not neglect time for yourself. Relaxation and self-care are crucial for maintaining a healthy balance.

- **Flexibility:** Be flexible and adjust your plan as needed. Life is unpredictable, so be ready to make adjustments.

- **Continuous Learning:** Constantly look for ways to improve your balance between career and personal life. Continuous learning is key to adapting to changes.

- **Support:** Seek support from family, friends, or a professional advisor if needed. Sometimes, having someone to talk to can make a difference.

Every individual has different needs, so it's important to find strategies that work best for you and your situation. Maintaining a balance between these different aspects of life will help you live more harmoniously and satisfactorily.

Technology and Digital Distraction

Modern technologies offer many opportunities but can also be a source of distraction and time loss. We will learn to use technology more consciously, reducing digital distractions and regaining control of our time.

Using technology more consciously and reducing digital distractions can significantly improve your control over your time. Here are some strategies:

- **Set Time Limits:** Use time control functions or apps to set limits on how much time you spend on certain apps or online activities. For example, you can use the "Screen Time" feature on iOS devices or time management apps like Forest.

- **Turn Off Non-Essential Notifications:** Minimize notifications on your phone or computer. Keep only essential ones, such as urgent messages or work communications, and disable notifications from social apps or games.

- **Organize Your Digital Workspace:** Keep your desktop and folders organized. Delete unnecessary files and neatly archive important documents. A clean digital environment helps reduce stress and distractions.

- **Set Dedicated Times:** Establish specific times for digital activities, such as managing emails or using social media. Stick to these times to avoid being online constantly.

- **Practice Digital Detox:** Dedicate regular periods during the day or week when you completely turn off digital devices. This can help you relax and reconnect with the real world.

- **Use Mindfulness Apps:** Apps like Headspace or Mindfulness can help reduce stress and increase awareness of your technology use.

- **Define Clear Goals:** Before starting a digital activity, set clear goals for what you intend to accomplish. This will help you stay focused on your mission.

- **Monitor Your Usage:** Use time tracking apps to monitor how much time you spend on different digital activities. This will give you a clear view of your usage patterns.

- **Involve Others:** Talk to friends or family and involve them in your commitment to use technology more consciously. They can help you stay accountable.

- **Reward Yourself:** After completing an important digital task or adhering to a time limit, reward yourself with a small treat to motivate you to maintain good habits.

Conscious use of technology requires practice and discipline, but it can lead to increased productivity, less stress, and better control of your time.

Planning and Deadline Management

Effective planning is crucial for making the most of the time available to us. We will explore planning and deadline management techniques to maintain organization and clarity in our lives.

Creativity and Free Time

The Right Balance is not only about work but also about creativity and free time. We will explore how to find time for creative passions and relaxation, contributing to our overall well-being.
Finding time for creative passions and relaxation is crucial for our

overall well-being. Here are some strategies:

- **Planning:** Allocate time in your schedule for creative passions and relaxation, just as you do for work commitments. Treat these moments with the same importance.

- **Simplicity:** Simplify your daily routine to free up space for creative activities and relaxation. Minimize non-essential activities or delegate them to others if possible.

- **Prioritization:** Recognize the importance of these activities for your well-being and prioritize them at the top of your list. This means saying "no" to commitments that can be sacrificed.

- **Time Management:** Use time management techniques, such as the "Pomodoro Technique," to intensely focus on creative passions for short periods and then allow yourself relaxation breaks.

- **Delegate and Involve Family:** If you have family commitments, involve your family in your creative passions or try to delegate some responsibilities to free up time.

- **Shared Hobbies:** Look for hobbies or creative activities that you can share with friends or family. This can make the time spent together even more valuable.

- **Digital Detox:** Reduce digital distractions and time spent on devices and social media. This will free up time for your passions.

- **Explore Short Activities:** You don't have to commit to long creative projects. Even short creative activities, such as painting or writing, can bring benefits.

- **Mindfulness:** Practice mindfulness to be more present in the moment and fully enjoy your creative and relaxation activities.

- **Self-Care:** Remember that taking care of yourself is essential for your overall well-being. Don't feel guilty about dedicating time to yourself.

Find the balance between your responsibilities and time for your creative passions and relaxation. This will significantly contribute to your physical and mental well-being.

Appreciating the Present Moment

Finally, we will learn the importance of living in the present moment. Often, we are so focused on the future or worried about the past that we lose sight of the present. We will find the Right Balance between planning for the future and appreciating the here and now.

This chapter is an invitation to explore how the Right Balance in time management can lead to a more balanced and productive life. We will learn to make the most of our time, reduce stress related to deadlines, and create space for enriching activities. The Right Balance in time management is the key to a more meaningful and less hectic life. Are you ready to begin the journey toward a more balanced and mindful use of your time?

Physical well-being is a fundamental component of our lives. The health of our body directly influences the overall quality of our existence. The Right Balance in this context teaches us to take care of our bodies without neglecting the satisfaction of our desires and pleasures.

Too often, the approach to health attention oscillates between excess and indifference. On one hand, we can become obsessed with physical perfection, following extreme diets and intense workouts. On the other hand, we can completely neglect our health, succumbing to poor eating habits and sedentary lifestyles. The Right Balance lies in the middle of these two extremes, where we find the ability to cultivate a healthy life without becoming obsessed with physical appearance.

A balanced diet is a key element of physical well-being. The Right Balance teaches us to choose nutritious foods that support our health, but also allows us to indulge in occasional pleasures without guilt. Moderation is the key. Eating mindfully, listening to our body and its needs, helps us maintain a healthy relationship with food.

Physical exercise is another pillar of well-being. The Right Balance suggests finding a balance between movement and rest. The importance of physical activity cannot be underestimated, but it is also essential to give the body time to recover and regenerate.

Quality rest and sleep are often overlooked in our hectic society. The Right Balance reminds us that sleep is essential for our physical and mental health. Taking time to rest is an act of authenticity and self-care for our bodies.

Physical well-being is not only about the body but also the mind and soul. Stress management, meditation, and mindfulness practice contribute to maintaining mental and emotional balance. Finally, self-compassion is a fundamental element of physical well-being. The Right Balance teaches us to treat our bodies with kindness and respect, accepting its limits and imperfections.

In the next chapter, we will explore the Right Balance in preparing for the future, showing how we can balance planning and preparation with the joy of the present. But first, reflect on your physical well-being. How can you apply the Right Balance to maintain a balance between caring for your body and satisfying your desires?

Chapter 8: The Right Balance in Ethics and Morality

Our ethical and moral conduct plays a fundamental role in our lives, shaping our decisions and actions. Too often, we find ourselves facing the dilemma between moral rigidity and ethical compromise. In this chapter, we will explore how to apply the concept of "The Right Balance" in the realm of ethics and morality, making thoughtful decisions and guiding our lives with wisdom.

Understanding Moral Differences

People have different ethical and moral perspectives, and The Right Balance requires the ability to understand and respect these differences. We will learn to navigate various ethical perspectives and find common ground.

To navigate various ethical perspectives and find common ground, it is important to follow some guidelines:

- **Study diverse ethical perspectives:** Begin by studying major ethical theories, such as deontological ethics, consequentialist ethics, and virtue ethics. Understanding the foundations of each perspective will help you see differences and similarities.

- **Active listening:** When engaged in ethical discussions, practice active listening. Seek to understand others' opinions without judgment. This fosters dialogue and mutual understanding.

- **In-depth research:** Before forming your own opinion, conduct in-depth research on a specific ethical topic. Examine arguments from different perspectives and evaluate evidence.

- **Create an open environment:** If involved in ethical discussions with others, create an open and respectful environment where each person can express their opinions without fear of judgment.

- **Identify common ground:** Look for commonalities among different perspectives. Often, even if ethical theories differ, there are shared values on which to build common ground.

- **Applied ethics:** Apply ethical theories to real-life situations. Ask yourself

which ethical perspective
provides the best solution
for a specific problem.

- **Compromise:** In some
  situations, you may need
  to seek a compromise
  between different ethical
  perspectives to find an
  acceptable common
  ground for everyone.

- **Continuous reflection:**
  Navigating ethical
  perspectives requires
  continuous reflection. Your
  opinions may evolve over
  time, so keep an open
  mind.

- **Intercultural dialogue:** If
  dealing with ethical issues
  in culturally diverse
  contexts, be sensitive to
  cultural differences and try
  to understand cultural
  perspectives.

- **Professional counseling:** In some complex situations, it might be helpful to consult ethical experts or advisors to assist in finding common ground.

Navigating ethical perspectives requires patience, open-mindedness, and a continuous commitment to constructive dialogue. Finding common ground can be challenging, but it is crucial for addressing complex ethical issues collaboratively and responsibly.

Ethical Flexibility and Personal Growth

Ethics is not an exact science but rather a field in constant evolution. We will explore how to be ethically flexible, allowing ourselves to grow and adapt to new information and challenges. Being ethically flexible is an important skill that allows us to grow and adapt to new information and challenges without compromising our core values. Here are some strategies to develop this ability:

- **Open-mindedness:** Be open to exploring new ideas and perspectives. Accept that your beliefs may change over time based on new information.

- **Self-reflection:** Regularly reflect on your ethical values and principles. Ask yourself why you believe in what you believe and if there is room for adjustments or evolution.

- **Active listening:** Listen carefully to others' opinions, even if they differ from your own. Try to understand their viewpoint and consider if there are valid elements in their arguments.

- **Ethical studies:** Deepen your study of ethics and ethical theories. This will help you better understand the foundations of your beliefs and explore new perspectives.

- **Constructive discussion:** Engage in constructive ethical discussions with others. This exposes you to diverse opinions and allows you to refine your positions.

- **Cognitive flexibility:** Develop the ability to adapt your thinking based on circumstances. Recognize that what is ethically right in one situation may not be in another.

- **Consequence evaluation:** Carefully consider the consequences of your actions and decisions in ethical terms. Ask yourself if your actions align with your values and those of the community you live in.

- **Feedback:** Seek feedback from friends, colleagues, or mentors on your ethical flexibility. Often, others can offer valuable perspectives.

- **Objectivity:** Strive to maintain an objective attitude in ethical situations, avoiding being influenced by emotions and personal biases.

- **Continuous learning:** Ethics is an evolving field. Keep learning and updating your ethical knowledge to stay informed about new challenges and developments.

Being ethically flexible does not mean compromising your values but rather being willing to explore and adapt consciously, allowing for personal growth and better addressing new ethical challenges.

Compassion and Forgiveness

The Right Balance in ethics also includes compassion and forgiveness. We will learn to be compassionate toward others and ourselves, understanding the transformative power of forgiveness.

Learning to be compassionate toward others and ourselves is an important process that can lead to a greater understanding of the transformative power of forgiveness. Here are some strategies to develop compassion and understand forgiveness:

- **Mindfulness practice:** Mindfulness is a practice that helps you be aware of the present moment in a non-judgmental way. This can foster compassion toward others and yourself by making you more attentive and present in relationships.

- **Empathy development:** Try to put yourself in others' shoes to understand their feelings and perspectives. Empathy is crucial for cultivating compassion.

- **Self-compassion practice:** Treat yourself with kindness and understanding. Don't be too harsh on yourself when you make mistakes or face challenges.

- **Understand forgiveness:** Study the concept of forgiveness and how it can lead to healing in relationships and emotional well-being. Forgiveness doesn't necessarily mean approving of behavior but freeing oneself from anger and resentment.

- **Active listening:** When someone approaches you with a problem or conflict, practice active listening. Show empathy and understand their emotions.

- **Use kind words:** Use kind and respectful words when addressing others and when talking to yourself. Avoid criticism and negative judgments.

- **Learn from past experiences:** Reflect on your past experiences of

forgiveness and
compassion. What have
you learned from them?
How can they guide you in
the future?

- **Personal growth:**
Understand that
compassion and
forgiveness are part of
personal growth. Accept
that it is an evolving
process.

- **Counseling or
psychotherapy:** In some
complex situations,
seeking the support of a
mental health professional
may be helpful to address
forgiveness and
compassion issues.

- **Share success stories:**
Listen to and share
success stories of
forgiveness and
compassion. This can

inspire you and provide
new perspectives.

Compassion and forgiveness can
lead to greater inner peace,
healthier relationships, and a
better understanding of the
transformative power of kindness
and understanding.

**Balancing Principles and
Practicality**

Making ethical decisions often
involves a balance between
principles and practicality. We will
explore how to find The Right
Balance between adhering strictly
to principles and adapting them
to circumstances.

Finding The Right Balance
between adhering strictly to
principles and adapting them to
circumstances is a complex
challenge that involves the virtue
of fairness and the ability to
discern. This concept has been
widely discussed in philosophy,

particularly by Aristotle. Here's how you can explore this idea:

- **Study Aristotle:** Aristotle introduced the concept of "ethical virtue" or "moderation" in his approach to ethics. Read works like "Nicomachean Ethics" to understand how he defines The Right Balance as the middle ground between extremes.

- **Apply discernment:** Develop the ability to discern when it is appropriate to adhere strictly to principles and when it is necessary to adapt them to circumstances. This requires wisdom and judgment.

- **Study historical examples:** Examine historical cases where fairness was successfully applied or lacked. Studying past situations can help you better evaluate current circumstances.

- **Reflect on your values:** Clarify your core values. This will help you establish guiding principles on which to base your decisions.

- **Practice flexibility:** Be willing to reconsider principles based on circumstances. Flexibility doesn't mean betraying your values but being open to nuances and exceptions.

- **Seek advice:** Talk to trusted individuals or mentors who have experience in finding The Right Balance. They can offer valuable perspectives.

- **Continuous reflection:** Take time for constant reflection on your decisions and the situations you find yourself in. Self-reflection helps develop the ability to adapt principles.

- **Practice compassion:** Consider others in your quest for The Right Balance. Compassion can help you find solutions that take into account others' needs and values.

- **Be open to change:** Circumstances change over time. Be open to reviewing and updating your principles based on new information and experiences.

- **Accept it as a process:** Finding The Right Balance is an evolving process.

Don't seek perfection but be willing to learn from mistakes and adapt to new challenges.

Finding The Right Balance requires time, practice, and self-awareness. It is an essential aspect of the virtue of fairness and ethics applied to everyday life.

Social Responsibility and Collective Impact

Our ethical actions have an impact on society and the community. We will learn to consider the effect of our choices on the entire community and find ways to contribute positively.
By exploring how to consider the effect of our choices on the entire community and contribute positively, we can adopt various strategies:

- **Ethical reflection:** Before making decisions, reflect on their possible consequences for the community. Evaluate whether your actions uphold ethical values such as justice, fairness, and solidarity.

- **Active involvement:** Actively participate in your community's life. Join local organizations, volunteer groups, or initiatives that promote the common good.

- **Education and awareness:** Inform yourself and others about the relevance of your choices. Organize events, workshops, or share information online to create awareness about the impacts of individual actions.

- **Support local initiatives:** Support local activities, small businesses, and locally produced goods. This can contribute to the local economy and strengthen the community.

- **Reduction of environmental impact:** Minimize your environmental impact through sustainable choices, such as recycling, energy conservation, and the use of public transport or bicycles.

- **Promotion of inclusion:** Advocate for social inclusion and against discrimination. Promote diversity and equal opportunities in your community.

- **Collaboration:** Work together with other community members to address common challenges and find solutions. Collaboration can lead to positive outcomes.

- **Improvement of education:** Invest in education, both personal and for others. Education is crucial for individual and collective progress.

- **Political participation:** Engage in the local political process by voting in elections and influencing the decisions of your representatives for the community's benefit.

- **Open communication:** Maintain open and respectful communication with other community members. Listen to their concerns and opinions.

- **In summary:** considering the effect of our choices on the community and contributing positively requires awareness, direct action, and cooperation with others. It is a constant commitment to improving collective well-being.

Integrity and Consistency

The Right Balance in ethics also includes integrity and consistency between our words and actions. We will explore how to live an ethical life where what we say aligns with what we do.
This chapter is a journey into the art of making thoughtful ethical decisions and leading a balanced moral life. We will learn to navigate the nuances of ethics, be compassionate and flexible, and guide our actions with integrity and wisdom. The Right Balance in ethics and morality is the key to an authentic and morally satisfying life. Are you ready to

begin this journey towards a balanced ethical and moral conduct?

Preparation for the Future

Preparation for the future is an inevitable part of life. We plan, save, and ensure we have a financial security plan to face the challenges that uncertainty may bring. However, the Right Balance teaches us to balance planning and preparation with the ability to enjoy the present and the joy of living.

It's essential to recognize that uncertainty is part of life itself. We cannot predict with certainty what the future holds, and attempting to control every detail can lead to feelings of anxiety and oppression. The Right Balance invites us to prepare for the future responsibly without being obsessed with the fear of the unknown.

One of the primary ways to apply the Right Balance in preparing for the future is through saving. Saving money is a wise and responsible practice, but it's crucial to do it in a balanced way. Too often, we focus exclusively on saving for the future, forgetting to enjoy the present. The Right Balance teaches us to find equilibrium between saving for the future and indulging in small pleasures in the present.

Personal financial management is another area where the Right Balance is crucial. The balance between saving and spending is delicate. The Right Balance encourages us to plan our finances responsibly, considering our future needs without neglecting our current well-being.

Future planning also involves preparing for emergencies. Having an emergency plan and a reserve fund can provide essential security in times of crisis.

However, it's equally important
not to live constantly in anxiety
about the uncertain future but to
live in the present with gratitude
and joy.

The Right Balance in this context
also teaches us to be flexible. Life
can bring unexpected changes,
and our ability to adapt to new
situations can be as important as
the planning itself.
Reflect on your preparation for
the future. How can you apply the
Right Balance to balance planning
and preparation with the joy of the
present?

Chapter 9: The Right Balance in Spiritual Well-Being

Spiritual well-being is an essential aspect of our lives that often gets overlooked in the modern era. Too frequently, we find ourselves navigating extremes, swinging between rampant materialism and hyper-spirituality. In this chapter, we will explore how to apply the concept of "The Right Balance" in spiritual well-being to achieve a profound connection with ourselves and the surrounding world without falling into spiritual excesses or rigidity.

Reflection and Meditation

Reflection and meditation are powerful tools for exploring our inner world. We will learn to find the Right Balance between contemplative silence and action in the world.

Exploring the Right Balance between contemplative silence and action in the world requires deep reflection and equilibrium. This challenge can be addressed by considering various aspects:

- **Balance between Solitude and Community:** Finding the right balance between moments of contemplative silence and active participation in the community is essential. Silence allows for reflection, while action promotes interaction with others.

- **Identifying Core Values:** Defining personal values and priorities helps guide choices. This enables a focus on actions that reflect deeply held principles.

- **Time Planning and Management:** Learning to manage time effectively is crucial. Allocate specific moments for silence and contemplation and others for action and social engagement.

- **Flexibility and Adaptability:** Being open to change and adapting to circumstances is essential. Sometimes, silence can inspire new modes of action, while experience in action can lead to deeper contemplation.

- **Self-Care and Well-Being:** Taking care of oneself is fundamental. Maintaining balance requires attention to physical and mental health through exercise, meditation, and other self-care practices.

- **Awareness of Impact:** Constantly reflecting on the effect of actions on the community and personal well-being. Ask whether actions align with life goals and collective well-being.

- **Continuous Learning:** Continuing to learn and grow in both contemplative silence and action. This fosters spiritual maturity and effectiveness in engaging with the world.

- **Sharing Experiences:** Sharing personal experiences with others can lead to new perspectives and approaches.

In conclusion, finding the Right Balance between contemplative silence and action in the world requires balance, awareness, and adaptability. It is an individual journey that can lead to a meaningful life and positive contribution to society.

Spiritual Sharing

Sharing spirituality with others is an important aspect of spiritual growth. We will explore how to connect with spiritual communities or sharing groups without losing our individuality. Connecting with spiritual communities or sharing groups without losing one's individuality is an important process that can enrich our spiritual and personal life. Here's how to do it:

- **Know Yourself:** Before seeking a community, it's crucial to have a clear understanding of who you are, your beliefs, and values. This will help you find a group that reflects your identity.

- **Conscious Research:** Look for communities or

groups that share your spiritual interests or personal goals. Research online, attend local events, or seek advice from trusted individuals.

- **Participate with Openness:** Once you find a group, participate with an open mind without losing your individuality. Maintain your beliefs and values and contribute with your unique perspectives.

- **Clear Communication:** Communicate openly with the group about your expectations and limits. Clear communication helps others understand your needs.

- **Balance Personal and Group Time:** Maintain a balance between time spent with the community and personal time for reflection and individual development.

- **Personal Growth:** View participation in a community as an opportunity for personal growth. Interactions with others can enrich your worldview and spirituality.

- **Maintain Authenticity:** Be authentic with yourself and other group members. Sincerity fosters meaningful connections.

- **Active Listening:** Practice active listening to understand others' experiences without judgment. This creates an environment of mutual acceptance.

- **Respect Differences:** Respect diverse opinions and perspectives within the group. Differences enrich the community.

- **Periods of Solitude:** Dedicate time to solitude and contemplation to maintain your inner connection.

In conclusion, connecting with a spiritual community or sharing group can enrich our lives, but it's essential to do so without losing our individuality. Balancing group membership with affirming personal identity is key to a positive and meaningful experience.

Nature and Spirituality

Connecting with nature can be a source of spiritual inspiration. We will learn to find the Right Balance between appreciating nature and being aware of ecology and sustainability.
Find the Right Balance between appreciating nature and being

aware of ecology and sustainability by following these steps:

- **Connection with Nature:** Dedicate time to connect with nature. Hikes, walks in parks, or simply moments of quietude outdoors can help develop a deep appreciation for the natural world.

- **Ecology Education:** Learn about ecology and sustainability. Read books, take online courses, or attend seminars to better understand how the ecosystem works and how your actions can influence it.

- **Reducing Environmental Impact:** Apply sustainable practices in your daily life. Reduce plastic consumption, save energy, support organic farming, and promote recycling.

- **Active Participation:** Join local groups or environmental organizations working for nature conservation and sustainability. Active participation connects you with like-minded individuals.

- **Sustainability in Daily Life:** Integrate sustainability into your daily life. Use public transportation or bicycles, reduce food waste, and support local and sustainable products.

- **Promoting Nature Appreciation:** Share your passion for nature with others. Organize hikes or outdoor events to invite friends and family to

discover the beauty of
nature.

- **Balance:** Find a balance between enjoying nature and contributing to its protection. You don't need to become a full-time environmental activist, but every small effort counts.

- **Appreciation of Natural Beauty:** Cultivate a deep appreciation for the beauty of nature. Photography, painting, or simply observing natural elements can strengthen your connection with the environment.

- **Continuous Learning:** Keep an open mind for learning and growth. Understanding ecology is an ongoing process.

- **Teaching Others:** Lastly, share your knowledge and experiences with others. Environmental education is crucial for promoting greater ecological awareness in society.

Find the Right Balance between appreciating nature and being aware of ecology and sustainability to live in harmony with the planet and contribute to its protection.

Compassion and Kindness

The Right Balance in spirituality also includes compassion and kindness towards others. We will explore how to cultivate compassion without becoming spiritual moralists.
Cultivating compassion without becoming spiritual moralists requires a balanced approach. Here's how to do it:

- **Understand Compassion:**
First and foremost,
understand that
compassion is the ability to
recognize others' suffering
without judgment or
condemnation. It's an act
of empathy and kindness.

- **Practice Mindfulness:**
Mindfulness meditation
can help develop an open
and compassionate mind.
This practice allows you to
observe your thoughts and
feelings without judgment,
making you more
empathetic towards
others.

- **Avoid Judgment:** Avoid
judging others or yourself.
Compassion involves
accepting human
imperfections. Focus on
understanding rather than
criticism.

- **Active Listening:** Practice active listening when someone shares their challenges or sufferings. Show genuine interest and empathy without trying to correct or give advice.

- **Be Kind to Yourself:** Compassion begins from within. Be kind and compassionate to yourself, accepting your mistakes and flaws. This will help you extend compassion to others.

- **Avoid Moralism:** Avoid becoming moralistic or imposing your spiritual views on others. Respect diverse perspectives and life choices.

- **Offer Support, Not Judgment:** When helping others, do so without conditions. Offer your support and kindness without judging whether their actions are "right" or "wrong."

- **Continuous Personal Growth:** Keep working on your personal and spiritual growth, but don't force others to follow your path. Everyone has their own time and journey.

- **Study Compassion:** Study and reflect on compassion through readings, lectures, or conversations with like-minded individuals.

- **Practice Gratitude:** Cultivate gratitude for people and experiences that teach you compassion. Recognizing what you've learned helps you genuinely cultivate compassion.

In summary, the key to cultivating compassion without becoming spiritual moralists is humility, listening, and accepting others. Compassion should be a freely given gift, not an imposed doctrine.

Spiritual Flexibility and Personal Growth

Our spirituality can evolve and change throughout life. We will learn to be flexible in our spiritual beliefs and use our spiritual quest as a tool for personal growth.

Flexibility in spiritual beliefs and using the spiritual quest as a tool for personal growth are practices that foster individual development. Here's how you can explore these dimensions:

- **Be Open to Spiritual Diversity:** Embrace the diversity of spiritual beliefs. Explore different religious traditions and life philosophies to gain broader perspectives.

- **Self-Reflection:** Spiritual exploration also means exploring yourself. Practice self-reflection to better understand your beliefs and personal values.

- **Spiritual Dialogue:** Engage in open and respectful spiritual dialogues with others. Listen to their experiences and share your own. This can lead to greater mutual understanding.

- **Welcome Spiritual Evolution:** Beliefs can evolve over time. Be open to changes in your spiritual beliefs without seeing them as a threat.

- **Explore Different Spiritual Practices:** Try various spiritual practices such as meditation, prayer, yoga, or mindfulness. Find what resonates most with you.

- **Spiritual Guidance:** If you seek spiritual guidance, look for a mentor or spiritual counselor who respects your needs and is open to your personal growth.

- **Develop Empathy:** Spiritual exploration can enhance empathy. Use this ability to connect deeply with others and support their spiritual growth.

- **Read and Study:** Read books, articles, and studies on spirituality and personal growth. This can enrich your understanding and offer new perspectives.

- **Practice Gratitude:** Develop a daily gratitude practice. Recognizing your spiritual blessings helps you grow internally.

- **Share Your Growth:** Don't keep your spiritual growth to yourself. Share it with others through teaching, art, writing, or support.

- **Be Patient:** Personal growth is a continuous journey. Be patient with yourself and allow your spiritual quest to unfold naturally.

Flexibility in beliefs and using the spiritual quest as a tool for personal growth can lead to greater wisdom, compassion, and self-awareness. These processes can enrich your life and understanding of the surrounding world.

Acceptance and Gratitude

Spiritual well-being often involves acceptance of what is and gratitude for what we have. We will explore how to practice acceptance and gratitude within the context of our spirituality. Practicing acceptance and gratitude within the context of spirituality can enrich our inner life and bring greater serenity. Here's how to do it:

- **Meditation and Mindfulness:** Meditation and mindfulness practices foster acceptance. Learn to observe your thoughts and emotions without judgment, accepting them as they are.

- **Acknowledge the Present Moment:** Focus on the present moment rather than worrying about the past or the future.

Recognize that the current moment is a gift.

- **Morning Gratitude:** Express gratitude for a new day upon waking. This can become a daily ritual to start the day with positivity.

- **Gratitude Journal:** Keep a journal where you write down things you're grateful for each day. This practice helps you focus on the blessings in your life.

- **Share with Others:** Sharing your gratitude with others can intensify it. Thank those you care about and perform acts of kindness.

- **Spiritual Growth:** In your spiritual quest, try to accept moments of doubt or difficulty as

opportunities for growth
and learning.

- **Prayer and Reflection:**
Use prayer or reflection as
moments to express
gratitude and acceptance
for the circumstances of
your life.

- **Nature Appreciation:**
Spend time in nature and
contemplate it. Observing
natural beauty can inspire
gratitude and acceptance.

- **Service to Others:**
Engage in serving others.
Helping others can
strengthen your sense of
gratitude for what you
have and acceptance of
challenges.

- **Spiritual Community:**
Participate in a spiritual
community or study group.
Sharing spiritual
experiences can

strengthen your sense of acceptance and gratitude.

- **Ceremonies and Rituals:** Attend ceremonies or spiritual rituals that emphasize acceptance and gratitude as fundamental values.

- **Personal Transcendence:** In your spiritual quest, try to transcend the ego and achieve a deeper understanding of your true nature.

- **Continuous Gratitude Practice:** Cultivate a consistent practice of acceptance and gratitude. This can become a significant part of your spirituality, bringing inner peace and a deeper connection with yourself, others, and the divine.

This chapter is an invitation to explore how the Right Balance in spiritual well-being can lead to a deeper and more meaningful life. We will learn to find our unique spiritual path, cultivate compassion and gratitude, and live a more balanced and centered life. The Right Balance in spiritual well-being is the key to a deeper connection with ourselves, others, and the world around us. Are you ready to embark on this journey towards balanced and meaningful spirituality?

Personal and spiritual growth is an intrinsic journey for every human being. It is the pursuit of knowledge, awareness, and meaning that enriches our inner life. The Right Balance in this context invites us to balance the desire for growth with inner peace and serenity.

In our fast-paced age, we are often driven to pursue personal growth incessantly, as if we must constantly improve ourselves. However, this approach can lead to a constant sense of dissatisfaction and perpetual anxiety. The Right Balance teaches us to cultivate personal growth in a balanced way, appreciating our progress without ever feeling incomplete.

Personal growth can take many forms, from continuous learning and reading to the pursuit of new skills and passions. The Right Balance lies in finding the right equilibrium between the desire to grow and accepting ourselves as we are. The importance of embracing our authenticity and not judging our worth solely based on achieved milestones.

The spiritual dimension is another aspect of personal growth that the Right Balance can enrich. The search for meaning and connection with something greater than ourselves is an essential part of life for many. The Right Balance in this context teaches us to explore spirituality in an open and respectful manner, without falling into religious extremism or complete lack of spirituality.

The practice of meditation and mindfulness can be a valuable tool for cultivating personal and spiritual growth through the Right Balance. These practices help us develop self-awareness and an understanding of the world around us, allowing us to deepen our connection with profound reality.

An attitude of gratitude is a key element of personal and spiritual growth through the Right Balance. Being grateful for what we have in life, for the lessons learned from challenges, and for daily joys can profoundly enrich our inner journey.

Reflect on your personal and spiritual growth. How can you apply the Right Balance to cultivate your knowledge, awareness, and meaning without losing inner peace?

Chapter 10: The Right Balance in Global Well-Being

Our lives are intertwined with the world around us, and our actions have a global impact. Too often, we find ourselves caught in a dichotomy between selfishness and the exclusive pursuit of personal well-being, and total sacrifice in the name of the common good. In this chapter, we will explore how to apply the concept of "The Right Balance" to global well-being, to positively contribute to society and the environment without compromising our personal well-being.

Global Awareness

Awareness of the world around us is the first step toward global well-being. We will learn to be informed about global issues, from climate change to social injustice, and understand how our daily actions have a global impact.

It is essential to be informed about global issues such as climate change and social injustice and understand how our daily actions have a global impact. Here's how to do it:

- **Education:** Inform yourself about global issues through reliable sources such as news, documentaries, and books. Follow organizations and experts dealing with these issues.

- **Active Participation:** Engage in local or online discussions and events on global issues. This will help you better understand the problems and potential solutions.

- **Reducing Ecological Footprint:** Reduce your environmental impact by adopting eco-friendly behaviors such as energy savings, waste reduction, and the use of sustainable transportation.

- **Sustainable Eating:** Choose local and seasonal foods, reduce meat consumption, and seek organic products. Agriculture significantly impacts climate change.

- **Supporting Charities:** Contribute financially or through volunteering to organizations fighting for environmental sustainability and social justice.

- **Online Activism:** Use social media to spread information and raise awareness about global issues. Your voice can make a difference.

- **Political Participation:** Vote for leaders who promote sustainable and fair policies. Influence change through your vote.

- **Continuous Education:** Keep informing yourself and learning about global issues. Awareness is the first step toward change.

- **Global Solidarity:** Understand that we are all interconnected, and your actions can impact people in other parts of the world. Develop empathy for global communities.

- **Sharing Knowledge:** Discuss global issues and the importance of daily actions with friends and family. Sharing knowledge is contagious.

Understanding the link between daily actions and global impact is essential to addressing global challenges. Each of us can contribute to a better world through informed and responsible choices.

Social and Environmental Responsibility

The Right Balance in global well-being also implies social and environmental responsibility. We will explore how we can make ethical and sustainable choices in consumption, production, and lifestyle.

Making ethical and sustainable choices in consumption, production, and lifestyle is crucial to contribute to a better world. Here's how you can do it:

- **Education and Awareness:** Learn about

ethical and environmental issues, such as production ethics, sustainable sourcing, and responsible brands. Knowledge is key to making informed decisions.

- **Responsible Consumption:** Practice conscious consumption. Buy local and seasonal products to reduce the environmental impact of transportation. Minimize waste and opt for durable products instead of disposable ones.

- **Sustainable Eating:** Reduce meat consumption and choose vegetarian or vegan options. This helps mitigate the environmental impact of the meat industry.

- **Energy and Resources:**
  Reduce energy
  consumption at home and
  use renewable energy
  sources. Recycle and
  reuse materials to
  contribute to waste
  reduction.

- **Sustainable Mobility:** Use
  public transportation,
  bicycles, or electric
  vehicles to reduce carbon
  emissions associated with
  travel.

- **Financial Sustainability:**
  Invest in ethical and
  sustainable financial
  products that promote
  responsible investment
  and environmental
  sustainability.

- **Supporting Responsible
  Brands:** Choose brands
  and companies that adopt
  ethical and sustainable
  production practices,

considering workers' rights and the environment.

- **Activism and Participation:** Join organizations and groups that promote sustainability and ethical consumption. Participate in local or global initiatives.

- **Innovation and Technology:** Support the development and adoption of sustainable technologies, such as solar energy and energy efficiency.

- **Sharing Knowledge:** Educate others about your ethical and sustainable choices. Sharing information can inspire positive changes in the community.

Your daily choices can have a significant impact on the planet and society. Choosing sustainability and ethics is a crucial step toward a better future for everyone.

Sharing and Volunteering

Contributing to society and the environment can bring profound satisfaction. We will learn to find the Right Balance in sharing resources and volunteering, making a meaningful contribution without depleting ourselves.

Find the Right Balance in sharing resources and volunteering to make a meaningful contribution without depleting yourself by following these tips:

- **Evaluate Your Resources:** Before committing to volunteering or sharing resources, realistically analyze your financial, physical, and time resources. Understand how much you can dedicate without jeopardizing your well-being.

- **Choose Your Passions and Skills:** Identify areas where you are most passionate and competent. Contributing to causes you care about will bring you greater satisfaction and prevent burnout.

- **Set Clear Limits:** Before starting a volunteering commitment or sharing, set clear limits on the time and resources you are willing to dedicate. Communicate these limits to the involved organizations or individuals.

- **Choose Reliable Organizations:** Look for organizations or groups with a reputation for transparency and efficiency in resource management. This will help ensure that your contribution has a positive impact.

- **Balance Giving and Receiving:** Don't forget to take care of yourself. Volunteering and sharing resources should bring joy and gratification but should not exhaust you completely. Find a balance between giving and receiving.

- **Flexibility in Commitment:** If you have intense periods at work or in your personal life, be flexible in volunteering commitment. Don't push yourself beyond your limits when you need time for yourself.

- **Continuous Training:** Seek opportunities for training and personal development to enhance your skills in volunteering or resource sharing. This will make you more effective in your contribution.

- **Recognition of Impact:** Monitor and celebrate the results of your commitment. Seeing the concrete positive effect of your contribution will motivate you to continue.

- **Networking and Support:** Seek support from other volunteers or individuals involved in resource sharing. Sharing experiences and challenges can be very helpful.

- **Recharge Your Energy:** Don't forget to take time for yourself to recharge when needed. Rest is essential for maintaining sustainable commitment.

The Right Balance lies in finding a balance between helping others and respecting yourself. With care and planning, you can make a meaningful contribution without depleting yourself.

Cooperation and Compassion

Global well-being also requires cooperation among individuals, communities, and nations. We will explore how to cultivate compassion and cooperation to address global challenges such as poverty, hunger, and environmental crises.

Cultivating compassion and cooperation to address global challenges such as poverty, hunger, and environmental crises is essential to promote a fairer and more sustainable world. Here's how you can contribute:

- **Education and Awareness:** Informing yourself about global challenges is the first step. Study and understand poverty, hunger, and environmental crises through resources such as UN reports, documentaries, and reliable news.

- **Promoting Compassion:** Try to develop empathy and compassion for those affected by these challenges. Imagine what it would be like to live in their situation and try to understand their needs.

- **Active Involvement:** Actively participate in volunteer initiatives or charitable organizations working to address these challenges. By contributing your time and resources, you can make a difference.

- **Advocacy:** Advocate for global issues. Use your voice to raise awareness among the public and political leaders on issues like poverty, hunger, and environmental crises. Participate in petitions, demonstrations, or lobbying for change.

- **Responsible Consumption:** Choose products and services that respect the environment and are produced ethically. Your purchasing power can influence company practices and promote sustainability.

- **Continuous Education:** Keep informing yourself and learning about these evolving challenges. Knowledge is the key to finding more effective solutions.

- **Global Collaboration:** Support international cooperation efforts and organizations working to address these challenges globally. Global challenges require global solutions.

- **Energy Conservation:** Reduce your environmental impact by cutting down on energy and water consumption, practicing recycling, and finding ways to reduce carbon emissions.

- **Education and Training:** Support education and training programs in communities affected by poverty. Education is a powerful means to break the cycle of poverty.

- **Community Awareness:** Involve your local community by organizing events, workshops, or discussions on these global challenges. Local awareness can lead to broader actions.

Compassion and cooperation are fundamental to addressing global challenges. Each of us can play a part in creating a fairer and more just world.

Acknowledging Disparities and Injustices

On the path to global well-being, it is important to acknowledge disparities and injustices in the world. We will learn to work towards equity and justice, seeking the Right Balance between personal change and collective action.

To promote equity and justice by seeking the Right Balance between personal change and collective action, it is important to adopt a balanced approach. Here are some steps you can teach your readers:

- **Understanding Equity and Justice:** Begin by educating your readers about the difference between equity (giving each what they need) and equality (treating everyone the same). Explain the importance of both perspectives.

- **Self-Reflection:** Encourage your readers to reflect on their own beliefs, privileges, and biases.

Personal change starts with self-awareness and openness to growth and learning.

- **Education and Awareness:** Provide resources and information to help your readers better understand issues related to equity and justice, such as racism, gender inequality, and poverty.

- **Small Daily Acts:** Show how small acts of kindness, understanding, and support for others can have a positive impact in promoting equity in everyday life.

- **Community Involvement:** Encourage collective action by participating in local initiatives or organizations working for social justice. Emphasize the importance of joining others to bring about meaningful change.

- **Advocacy and Activism:** Teach your readers how they can become activists or advocates for causes that promote equity and justice. Explain how to engage in campaigns, petitions, and protests for change.

- **Open Dialogue:** Promote open dialogue and constructive confrontation. Invite your readers to listen to diverse perspectives and seek collaborative solutions.

- **Supporting Institutional Change:** Illustrate the importance of supporting systematic and institutional changes to address equity issues. These changes may include legislative and policy reforms.

- **Persistence and Patience:** Emphasize that the path to equity and justice is often long and requires time. Encourage persistence and patience in pursuing these goals.

- **Sharing Success Stories:** Share stories of individuals or communities that have made a difference through their commitment to equity and justice. These stories will inspire your readers.

Remind your readers that the Right Balance between personal change and collective action is crucial to creating a fairer and more just world. Everyone can contribute significantly when acting in harmony with others for the common good.

Sustainability and the Future of the Planet

Finally, we will explore how global well-being is linked to the long-term sustainability of our planet. We will learn to find the Right Balance between responsible consumption and the conservation of natural resources for future generations.

This chapter is an invitation to explore how the Right Balance in global well-being can lead to a more meaningful life and harmony with the world. We will learn to contribute positively to society and the environment without compromising our personal well-being. The Right Balance in global well-being is the key to living a life with a greater purpose and a deeper connection to the world around us. Are you ready to start this journey toward a balanced and meaningful global well-being?

The present is where life unfolds.
However, too often, we are
engrossed in thoughts of the past
or anxious about the future,
overlooking the beauty and
richness of the present moment.
The Right Balance in this context
teaches us to live with awareness
and gratitude, to fully enjoy each
moment without losing sight of
the past or the future.

Life is a series of moments, each
with its uniqueness and value.
Yet, we are often so distracted by
past worries or future concerns
that we fail to fully perceive the
present. The Right Balance invites
us to slow down, to breathe
deeply, and to immerse ourselves
in the details of the present
moment.

One of the primary practices for
living in the present is
mindfulness or awareness. This
practice teaches us to be fully
present, to perceive our thoughts,
emotions, and bodily sensations

without judgment. Mindfulness helps us connect with the present moment deeply and meaningfully.

Gratitude is another essential element for living in the present through the Right Balance. Being grateful for what we have in life, for the people we love, for the small daily joys, helps us recognize the value of the present moment. Gratitude can transform our perspective, leading us to see beauty even in seemingly ordinary things.

The Right Balance also teaches us to let go of the past and not worry excessively about the future. The past cannot be changed, and excessive rumination on past mistakes can prevent us from living in the present. At the same time, anxiety about the future can prevent us from fully enjoying what we have today. The Right Balance lies in balancing reflection on the past with the joy of the present and responsible preparation for the future.

Simplicity is another key principle in living in the present through the Right Balance. Often, we are surrounded by excessive distractions that prevent us from focusing on the present moment. Finding beauty in the simplicity of everyday life can deeply enrich our relationship with the present.

In the next chapter, we will explore the Right Balance in lasting happiness, showing how we can find joy and satisfaction in daily life through the application of this philosophy. But first, reflect on your relationship with the present. How can you apply the Right Balance to live more mindfully and gratefully in every moment of your life?

Lasting Happiness: The Right Balance in Daily Life

Happiness is a goal that many of us constantly pursue. However, often our search for happiness is based on misconceptions or superficial goals that leave us dissatisfied in the long run. The Right Balance teaches us how to find joy and deep satisfaction in daily life.

Lasting happiness is not tied to external circumstances such as success, wealth, or social recognition. It is rather an intrinsic quality that can be cultivated through the practice of the Right Balance. This path to happiness involves a series of key principles.

One of the fundamental principles is gratitude. Being grateful for what we have in life helps us focus on what is positive and meaningful. Gratitude allows us to recognize the beauty of small things and to appreciate the present.

Mindfulness is another crucial practice for cultivating happiness through the Right Balance. It teaches us to be present in the moment, to live each instant with awareness, and not to allow negative or anxious thoughts to dominate our minds.

Compassion is a key element of lasting happiness. Being kind and compassionate towards others, as well as towards ourselves, creates a sense of connection and deep satisfaction. The ability to understand the pain and suffering of others helps us cultivate empathy and solidarity.

The Right Balance also teaches us to find happiness in simplicity. We don't have to seek happiness in material purchases or external success. Instead, we can find joy in the simplest things, such as an outdoor walk, a meaningful conversation, or a moment of tranquility.

Acceptance is another fundamental aspect of lasting happiness through the Right Balance. Accepting ourselves and others with all imperfections and weaknesses allows us to live with greater lightness and satisfaction.

Finally, lasting happiness involves the search for deeper meaning in life. Identifying our values and purposes, and acting in line with them, can lead to a sense of fulfillment and contentment.
In the next chapter, we will conclude our journey through the Right Balance, summarizing the key principles and offering an invitation to apply this philosophy in your daily life. But first, reflect on your pursuit of happiness. How can you apply the Right Balance to find lasting joy and satisfaction in your life?

Conclusion: Embracing the Right Balance in Life

In this journey through the concept of "The Right Balance," we have explored how to find equilibrium and harmony in all spheres of our lives. We have seen how applying this philosophy can lead to a more satisfying, meaningful, and fulfilling life. The Right Balance does not signify mediocrity or surrender but rather the pursuit of a dynamic balance between extremes, a middle path that allows us to make the most of life.

You have learned how to apply the Right Balance in your career, interpersonal relationships, health and well-being, personal growth, ethics and morality, spiritual well-being, and global well-being. Now is the time to put these lessons into practice in your life.

Call to Action: Find Your Right Balance

We challenge you to find your Right Balance in every aspect of your life. There is no universal formula, but rather a unique path that you must chart. Here are some concrete actions you can take:

- **Reflect:** Take time to reflect on which areas of your life could benefit from applying the Right Balance. It could be the balance between work and personal life, time management, your personal growth, or other aspects.

- **Define Your Values:** What are your core values? What is truly important to you? These values will be the compass guiding you in the search for the Right Balance.

- **Be Flexible:** Remember that life is constantly evolving. Be open to changing your approach and seeking new balances depending on circumstances.

- **Practice Mindfulness:** Self-awareness and awareness of the world around you are crucial. Learn to pay attention to your actions, decisions, and their consequences.

- **Share and Collaborate:** Involve others in your journey towards the Right Balance. Sharing experiences and challenges can lead to a deeper understanding and new perspectives.

- **Grow Constantly:** Personal growth is an endless journey. Be open

to learning and growing
continuously, adjusting
your Right Balance along
the way.

Find your Right Balance and
watch how your life becomes
enriched with meaning and
equilibrium. Remember that there
is no right or wrong answer, but
rather a unique path that is yours
and yours alone. Embrace the
Right Balance and discover a life
of harmony, satisfaction, and
fulfillment.